MUTTS

SUNDAYS

By Patrick McDonnell

Andrews McMeel
Publishing

Kansas City

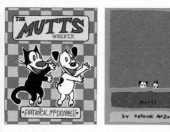

MUTTS is distributed internationally by King Features Syndicate, Inc. For information write King Features Syndicate, Inc., 235 East 45th Street, New York, New York 10017.

www.andrewsmcmeel.com   MUTTS SUNDAYS is printed on recycled paper.

99 00 01 02 03 BAM 10 9 8 7 6 5 4 3 2 1

ISBN: 0-7407-0010-3

Library of Congress Catalog Card Number: 99-61210

Thanks to Stephanie Bennett, Jay Kennedy, Frank Caruso, Doug Wong, Tim Rosenthal, Jim Keefe, Mark Tonra, Robert McDonnell, Danny Misdea, Marie, Mac, and Karen.

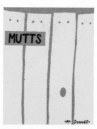

TO JAMES SWINNERTON, RICHARD OUTCAULT,
WINSOR McCAY, LYONEL FEININGER, BILLY DE BECK
PERCY CROSBY, CLIFF STERRETT, HAROLD GRAY,
CHESTER GOULD, ERNIE BUSHMILLER, WALT KELLY,
ELZIE SEGAR, GEORGE HERRIMAN,
AND CHARLES M. SCHULZ.

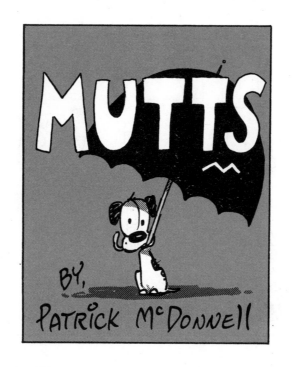

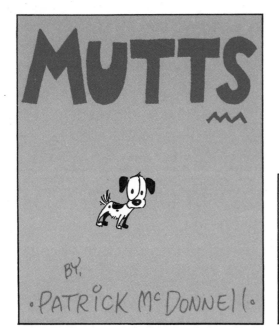

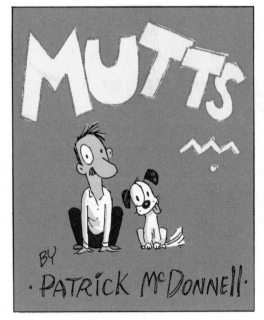

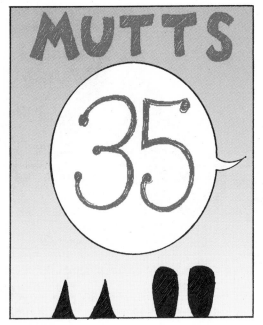

13

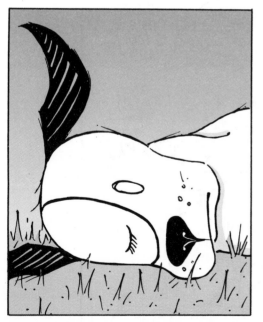

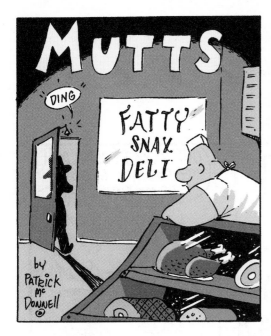

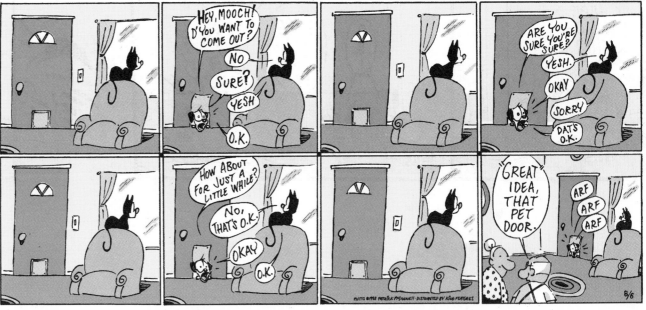

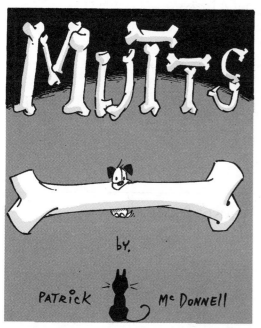

26

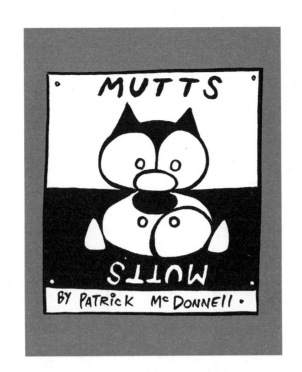

mutts

• by PATRICK McDONNELL •

33

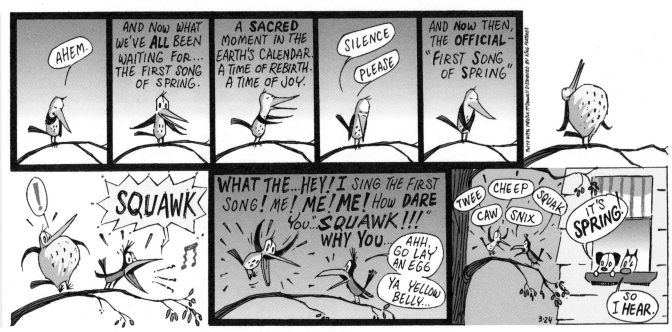

40

41

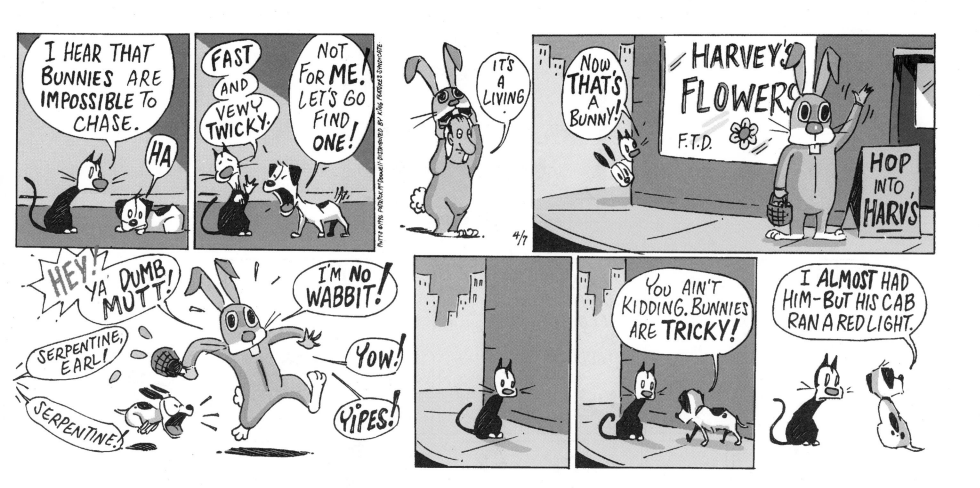

43

45

47

HOOOWL   HOOOWL

WHAT'S WITH ALL THE BLUBBERING, ~BOYS?
WE WERE MISSING OUR **MOMS**.
WATSIT TO YA?

OH, MUMSHY...DEVOTED, LOVING **MAW!** *SHE* WHO CARRIED ME BY THE SHCRUFF OF MY WITTLE NECK; **SHE** WHO LICKED MY DIRTY WITTLE FACE; **SHE** WHO PURRED ME TO SHWEET, SHWEET SLEEP...

OH, I MISH HER SO...
I MISH THAT SO...

AIN'T **NOBODY HERE** GOING TO LICK THAT DIRTY WITTLE FACE **TODAY**, PAL...

HOOWL

5/12

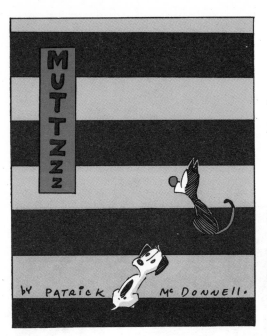

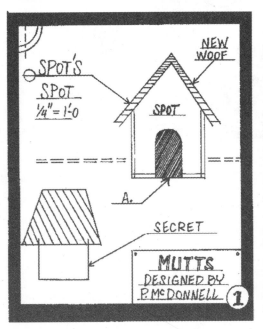

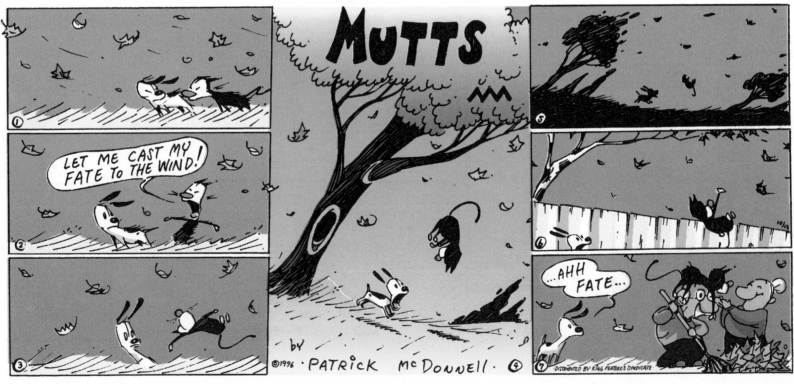

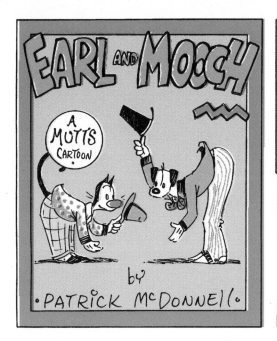

62

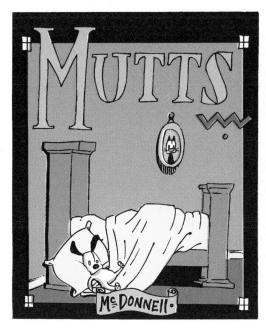

MUTTS

· PATRÍCK McDONNEll ·

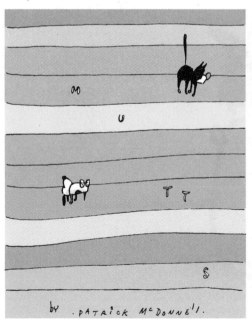

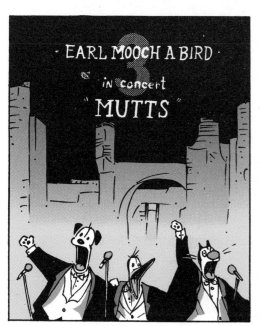

MUTTS
by
Patrick
McDonnell

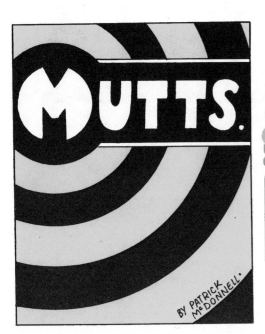

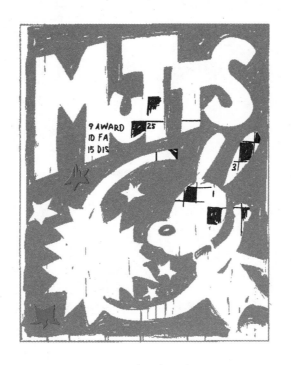

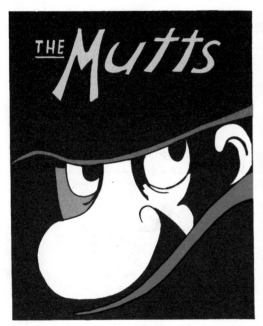

MUTTS

ROUND UP THE USUAL SUSPECTS AND MEET ME AT THE COURTHOUSE

OKAY, CHIEF!

CRIMESHTOPPERS TEXTBOOK

SHTAY OFF THE SHOFA!

· ROGUES GALLERY ·

FLATTAB LITTLEFACE KITTY SHMUMBLES PRUNEPUSS

MUTTS ©1997 PATRICK MCDONNELL · DISTRIBUTED BY KING FEATURES SYNDICATE

WHAT DID THEY **DO**?

THEY'RE CATS! THEY'RE **ALL** GUILTY OF SOMETHING!

I'LL GET 'EM TO CONFESS. OKAY, BOYS— **START** SINGING!

MEOOWR! MEEOOW!

THEN **WHAT** HAPPENED?

THE **JUDGE** THREW THE **BOOK** AT THEM.

10·5

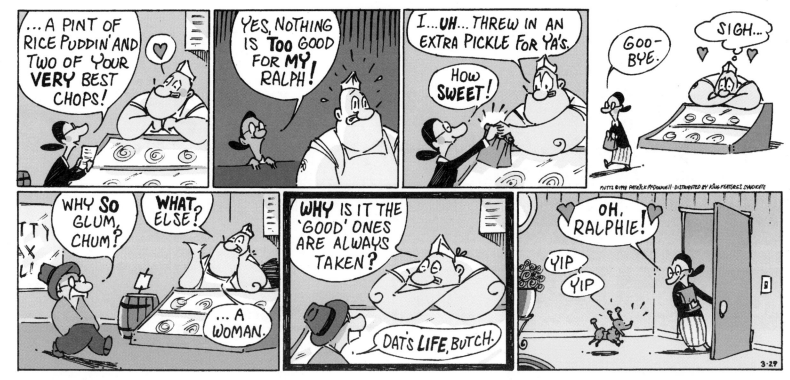

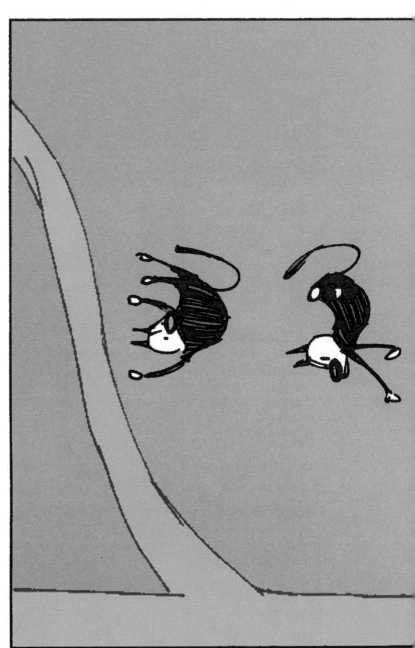

116

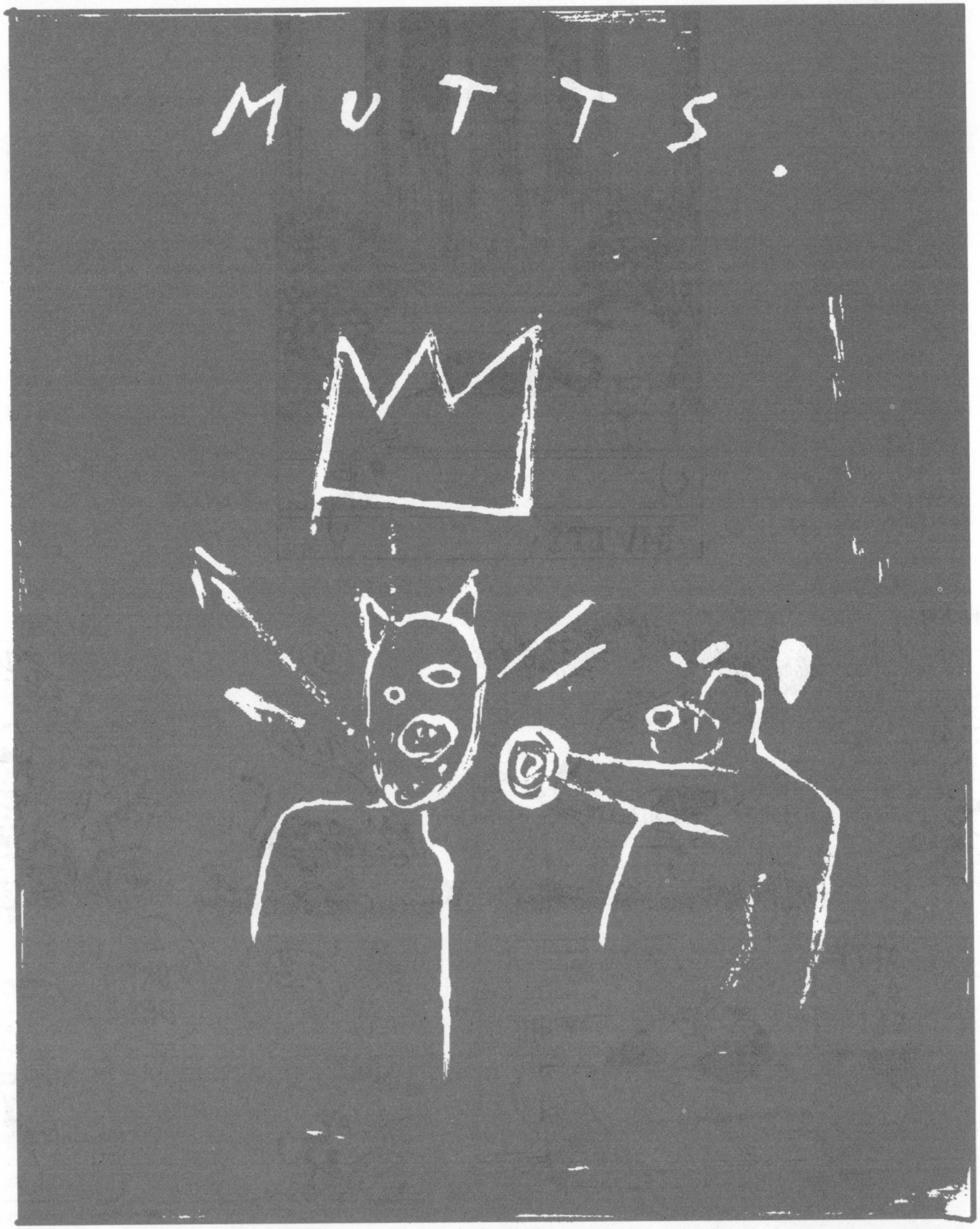
MUTTS.

Mutts.

BEWARE OF DOG

BEWARE OF DOG

BEWARE OF DOG

BEWARE OF DOG

I MIGHT BREAK YOUR HEART.

COMICS

BY PATRICK McDONNELL

STAY.

SIT! SHTAY! SHPEAK!!! WHAT'S NEXT? "EARL, DO MY LAUNDRY."!?!

BROTHER! ARE YOU DOMESHTICATED OR WHAT!?!

THEY'RE GONNA KEEP ON BREEDING YOU UNTIL YA COME OUT WITH A LI'L BUTLER'S OUTFIT—THE PERFECT DOG!

DOGS!!! HAVE YOU NO PRIDE!!! CAN'T YOU THINKS FOR YOURSHELF!!!

GOOD BOY! HERE'S A TREAT FOR

YOU.

NOPE. I DON'T HAVE A THOUGHT IN MY WITTLE FUZZY HEAD... OH, PWEASE MASHTER, TELL ME WHAT TO DO...

HEY!

I SHTAYED TOO!

9·13

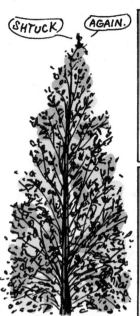

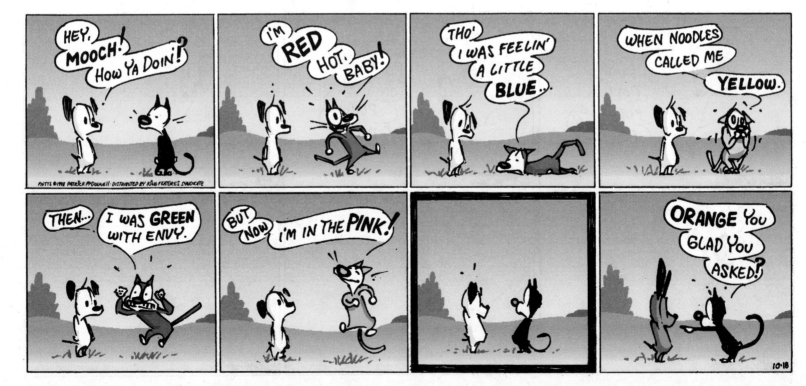

"Hi, SHTINKY" "WHERE YA GOING?"

"I'VE GOT TO VISIT MY ANGELS" "ANGELS!!?!"

NOT TOO LONG AGO... I WAS LOST... ALONE... HUNGRY... SCARED...

THEN OUT OF NOWHERE... THEY APPEARED!

ONE FED ME...   ONE WASHED ME...   ONE FIXED UP MY BUSTED LEG...   THEY ALL HELD ME...  SO I WOULDN'T FEEL SO ALONE IN THIS BIG OL' WORLD...

THEN BEYOND ALL MIRACLES—THEY FOUND ME MY "ANNIE"!

"YUP." "ANGELS. I SAY!"

"PURRRR..."

ANIMAL SHELTER

SUPPORT YOUR LOCAL SHELTER

MUTTS ©1998 PATRICK McDONNELL · DISTRIBUTED BY KING FEATURES SYNDICATE 11-1

MUTTS.